WIRED TO WIN - THE OFFICIAL SUCCESS DOCTRINE

WORKBOOK

A Practical Guide to Living a Life of Victory

Robert L. Wood, MBA

ISBN for Paperback: 979-8-9933082-2-7

Disclaimer:

This workbook is intended to support your personal growth and learning journey. The exercises and strategies provided are for self-improvement purposes and are not a replacement for professional, legal, financial, or therapeutic advice. The author and publisher disclaim any liability arising directly or indirectly from the use or application of the information in this workbook. Please use your own judgment and consult qualified professionals when needed.

Preface:

Your Journey Begins Here

This workbook is your companion to *Wired to Win*. It is designed to transform the book's powerful principles from concepts you understand into practices you live by. Each workshop corresponds to key chapters, pushing you to reflect, plan, and act.

True change requires more than reading; it requires doing. This is your space to do the work. Let's begin.

Table Of Contents

SECTION I

The Foundation -
The Winning Mindset

WORKSHOP 1:
The Success Doctrine - Are You Truly Wired to Win?

Objective:

To conduct an honest self-assessment of your current relationship with "winning" and define what it must mean for you moving forward.

A. Reflection: Your Winning History

1. How did you learn to define "winning" as a child? Was it about grades, sports, approval, or something else?

_____

_____

_____

2. Describe a time you achieved a significant "win." How did it feel? Did the feeling last?

_____

_____

_____

3. Describe a time you experienced a significant "loss." What did you learn about yourself from that experience?

_____

_____

_____

B. Exercise: The Winning Wiring Audit

Rate yourself on a scale of 1 (Not at all) to 5 (Absolutely) for the following statements:

- I believe I am capable of achieving extraordinary things. (1 - 2 - 3 - 4 - 5)
- I have a clear picture of what I want my life to look like in 5 years. (1 - 2 - 3 - 4 - 5)
- When I face an obstacle, my first instinct is to find a way around it. (1 - 2 - 3 - 4 - 5)
- I consistently follow through on my commitments to myself. (1 - 2 - 3 - 4 - 5)
- I see setbacks as necessary feedback, not final failure. (1 - 2 - 3 - 4 - 5)

Analysis: Where did you score lowest? That area is your greatest opportunity for growth in this program.

- **Area for Growth:**_____

_____

_____

C. Action: Redefining Winning

Based on your reflections, write your new, personal definition of winning. It must be on your own terms.

- **"For me, winning is no longer about**_____. **True winning is about**

_____**."**

Born Wired to Win - Embracing Your Innate Potential

> **Objective:**
> To dismantle the myth of being "average" and reconnect with your unique, inherent capacity for success.

A. Reflection: The "Average" Lie

1. In what areas of your life have you settled for "average" or "good enough"? Why?

_____

_____

_____

2. What is one unique talent, perspective, or experience you possess that others don't?

_____

_____

_____

3. How have your past struggles or "scars" actually given you wisdom or strength?

_____

_____

_____

B. Exercise: Your Potential Circuit

Imagine your potential is an electrical circuit. Answer the following:

- **Where is the power source strongest in my life?** (What energizes me?)

  _____

  _____

- **Where are the connections clear?** (What activities feel effortless and aligned?)

  _____

  _____

- **Where is there "corrosion" like fear, doubt, or lack of clarity?** (What blocks my energy?)

  _____

  _____

C. Action: The "Not Average" Declaration

Write a declaration that celebrates your non-averageness. Be specific.

- **Example:** "I am not average because my ability to_____combined with my experience of_____ makes me uniquely qualified to_____."

- **My Declaration:** "I am not average because..."_____

  _____

  _____

  _____

  _____

Mindset Matters - The Fixed vs. Growth Mindset Audit

Objective:

To identify fixed mindset thinking and learn to systematically shift it to a growth mindset.

A. Reflection: Mindset Triggers

1. What is a recent challenge where you noticed a fixed mindset voice (e.g., "I can't do this," "It's too hard")?

_____

_____

_____

_____

2. What is an area where you naturally have a growth mindset? (e.g., "I can learn this new software," "I can get better at cooking")?

_____

_____

_____

_____

B. Exercise: The Mindset Journal

For one week, keep a log. When you face a challenge, write down:

- **The Situation:**
- **Fixed Mindset Voice:**
- **Growth Mindset Reframe:**

Day	Situation	Fixed Mindset Voice	Growth Mindset Reframe
Mon			
Tue			
Wed			
Thu			
Fri			
Sat			
Sun			

C. Action: The Growth Question

Commit to asking yourself this question when you face a setback: "What is this situation trying to teach me?" Make this your automatic response to difficulty.

SECTION II

The Blueprint -
Vision, Mission & Goals

The Power of Vision - Crafting Your Compelling Future

Objective:

To move beyond vague dreams and create a multi-sensory, emotionally compelling vision that pulls you forward.

A. Reflection: The Clarity Gap

1. If you continued on your current path, where would you be in 5 years?

_____

_____

_____

_____

2. Where would you love to be in 5 years? What is the gap between these two answers?

_____

_____

_____

_____

B. Exercise: The Vivid Vision Exercise

Find a quiet space. Close your eyes and imagine your ideal life 5 years from now. Engage all your senses. Then, write a detailed description answering these questions:

- **What do you SEE?** (Your environment, your workspace, the people around you)

_____

_____

- **What do you HEAR?** (Words of encouragement, sounds of your success, laughter)

_____

_____

- **What do you FEEL?** (Emotionally: pride, peace, excitement. Physically: energy, health)

_____

_____

- **What are you DOING?** (Describe a typical day)

_____

_____

C. Action: Vision Statement

Condense your vivid vision into one powerful sentence.

- **My Vision Statement:** "My vision is to live a life of [core value] where I [primary action] resulting in [primary impact/feeling]."

    o Example: "My vision is to live a life of creative freedom where I empower others through teaching, resulting in a legacy of inspired action."

◉ o **Your Vision**

Statement: _____

_____

_____

_____

_____

_____

_____

_____

Defining the Win - Creating Your Personal Constitution

Objective:

To create a personal mission statement that acts as a decision-making filter and a source of motivation.

A. Reflection: Core Values

1. What 3-5 values are non-negotiable in your life? (e.g., Integrity, Family, Growth, Service, Freedom)

1. _____

2. _____

3. _____

4. _____

5. _____

2. What does "a life well-lived" mean to you?

_____

_____

_____

_____

B. Exercise: Draft Your Personal Constitution

Your constitution has three parts:

1. **Preamble (Who I Am):** I am a [values-based identity]. (e.g., I am a man of integrity and growth.)

2. **Articles (What I Do):** I am committed to [key actions]. (e.g., I am committed to lifelong learning and serving my family.)

3. **Amendments (My Boundaries):** I will not [compromise my values]. (e.g., I will not sacrifice my health for temporary success.)

4. **My Draft Personal Constitution:**

   o   Preamble:_____

   o   Articles:_____

   o   Amendments:_____

C. Action: Constitutional Test

Review your constitution. Is it clear, compelling, and easy to remember? Refine it until it feels powerful. This is your personal rule of law.

Goals - The Anatomy of a Well-Designed Goal

Objective:

To master the art of setting goals that are strategic, motivating, and achievable.

A. Reflection: Past Goal Analysis

1. What is a goal you set and achieved? What made it successful?

_____

_____

_____

_____

2. What is a goal you set and failed to achieve? What were the obstacles?

_____

_____

_____

_____

B. Exercise: The S.M.A.R.T. ER Goal Framework

Go beyond S.M.A.R.T. (Specific, Measurable, Achievable, Relevant, Time-bound) by adding:

- Exciting (Does it inspire you?)

- Reviewed (How will you track progress?)

Apply this framework to a current goal:

- **Specific:** What exactly will you accomplish?

- **Measurable:** How will you measure success?

- **Achievable:** Is it realistic yet challenging?

- **Relevant:** Does it align with your vision and constitution?

- **Time-bound:** What is the deadline?

- **Exciting:** Why does this goal matter to you on an emotional level?

- **Reviewed:** How often will you check progress? (Weekly? Monthly?)

- **My S.M.A.R.T. ER Goal:** _____

_____

_____

_____

C. Action: Goal Alignment Check

Take your S.M.A.R.T. ER goal and ask: Does achieving this goal directly move me toward my Vision Statement? If not, revise the goal until it does.

_____

_____

_____

_____

SECTION III

The Engine - Discipline, Habits & Resilience

WORKSHOP 7:

Discipline - Forging the Bridge to Victory

— Objective: —

To understand discipline as a loving practice of self-accountability, not punishment, and to build a personal discipline plan.

A. Reflection: Discipline vs. Motivation

1. When has motivation failed you? Describe the situation.

_____

_____

_____

_____

2. When has discipline carried you through? What did that feel like?

_____

_____

_____

_____

B. Exercise: The Discipline Dashboard

Evaluate your current discipline level in key areas (1=Low, 5=High):

Area of Life	Current Discipline (1-5)	One action to improve
Health (Sleep, Diet, Exercise)		
Finances (Budgeting, Saving)		
Learning (Reading, Skills)		
Relationships (Communication, Time)		
Work/Career		

C. Action: The Discipline Promise

Choose the area with the lowest score. Make one specific, non-negotiable promise to yourself for the next 7 days.

- **"For the next 7 days, I promise myself I will [specific action] no matter what."**

_____

_____

_____

_____

_____

_____

_____

The Discipline of Habits - Building Systems for Success

Objective:

To design a system of habits that automate progress toward your goals.

A. Reflection: Habit Audit

1. What is one daily habit that serves you well?

_____

_____

_____

_____

2. What is one habit that undermines your goals?

_____

_____

_____

_____

B. Exercise: Habit Stacking Design

Use the formula: "After [CURRENT HABIT], I will [NEW HABIT]."

- **Example:** "After I pour my morning coffee, I will write for 15 minutes."
- **Design 3 Habit Stacks:**

1. After_____, I will_____

2. After_____, I will_____

3. After_____, I will_____

C. Action: The 30-Day Habit Challenge

Pick one new habit stack. Commit to it for 30 days. Use a calendar to track your streak. The goal is not perfection, but consistency. Never miss twice.

Resilience -
The Art of the Comeback

Objective:

To develop a personalized resilience strategy for bouncing back from setbacks stronger than before.

A. Reflection: The Clarity Gap

1. Who do you know that is highly resilient? What do they do when faced with adversity?

_____

_____

_____

_____

2. What was your greatest comeback? What did it teach you about your own strength?

_____

_____

_____

_____

B. Exercise: The Resilience Toolkit

Create a go-to list of actions for when you get knocked down.

- **Physical Reset:** (e.g., 10-minute walk, deep breathing, workout)

  _____

  _____

- **Mental Reframe:** (e.g., Journaling, asking "What can I learn?", talking to a mentor)

  _____

  _____

- **Spiritual Recharge:** (e.g., Prayer, meditation, reading inspiring stories)

  _____

  _____

- **Social Support:** (e.g., Call a specific friend, attend a support group)

  _____

  _____

C. Action: Pre-Mortem Planning

Pick an important goal. Now, imagine it fails. Why did it fail? Write down the potential reasons. Then, for each potential failure, write a contingency plan. This prepares you for obstacles before they happen.

SECTION IV

The Amplifiers - Leadership, Community & Legacy

Leadership from the Inside Out - Leading Yourself First

⧓

Objective:

To recognize that all leadership begins with self-leadership and to assess your leadership in key areas of your life.

A. Reflection: The Leadership Void

1. Where in your life or community do you see a need for better leadership?

_____

_____

_____

_____

2. When have you taken responsibility when you didn't have to? What was the outcome?

_____

_____

_____

_____

B. Exercise: The Self-Leadership Scorecard

Rate yourself (1=Needs Work, 5=Excellent) on these pillars of self-leadership:

- **Vision Casting:** I clearly see and communicate where I'm going. (1-2-3-4-5)
- **Integrity:** My actions match my words, especially in private. (1-2-3-4-5)
- **Accountability:** I take responsibility for my results and mistakes. (1-2-3-4-5)
- **Courage:** I make tough decisions and have difficult conversations. (1-2-3-4-5)
- **Service:** I look for ways to add value to others. (1-2-3-4-5)

C. Action: The 1% Improvement Challenge

Choose your lowest-scoring pillar. What is one small way you can improve by just 1% this week? (e.g., If Integrity is low: "I will be 5 minutes early to every appointment this week.")

The Power of Mentorship & Being a Mentor

Objective:

To understand the dual role of a mentor and a mentee, and to create a plan for both seeking guidance and offering it.

A. Reflection: The Guidance in Your Life

1. Who has informally or formally mentored you in the past? What was the most valuable lesson they imparted?

_____

_____

_____

2. What is a specific challenge you are currently facing where a mentor's perspective would be invaluable?

_____

_____

_____

3. When have you found yourself naturally offering advice or guidance to someone else? What does that topic say about your own areas of strength?

_____

_____

_____

B. Exercise: The Mentor Map

1. **Seeking a Mentor:** Identify 2-3 potential mentors whose life or career reflects results you admire.

- o Name:_____. Area of Expertise:_____

- o Name:_____. Area of Expertise:_____

- o **My "Mentor Ask" Script:** Draft a concise, respectful request for a small amount of their time, being specific about what you need.

  "Hello [Name], I greatly admire your work in [specific area]. I am focused on growing in this area myself and would be grateful for the opportunity to ask you for 20 minutes of your time to discuss [one specific challenge]."

My Script:_____

_____

_____

1. **Becoming a Mentor:** Identify who you could mentor. This isn't about being an expert, but about being one step ahead.
   - o Who is watching you? Who could benefit from the lessons you've already learned?
   - o My "Mentoring Offer": How could I offer support? (e.g., "I noticed you're working on X. I went through something similar; I'd be happy to share what worked for me.")

   _____

   _____

   _____

C. Action: The First Step

This week, take one action from your Mentor Map. Send one email to a potential mentor, or have one conversation where you offer genuine, non-condescending advice to someone who could benefit.

The Community Factor - Building Your Winning Tribe

⁓⁓⁓

Objective:

To strategically assess and build a personal and professional community that actively supports your growth and success.

A. Reflection: Your Current Ecosystem

1. After spending time with your different friends or groups, do you feel energized and elevated, or drained and diminished?

_____

_____

_____

_____

2. What "shared vision" does your primary community have? Is it aligned with growth, or something else?

_____

_____

_____

_____

B. Exercise: The Tribe Audit

Create a three-tiered map of your community:

- **The Inner Circle (The Council):** These are your 3-5 people. They know your vision, hold you accountable with love, and are your first call in a crisis. Write their names and what they contribute to your life.

  1._____| Contribution:_____

  2._____| Contribution:_____

  3._____| Contribution:_____

- **The Affiliate Circle (The Allies):** These are positive connections, colleagues, and acquaintances. The interaction is mutually beneficial and generally positive. They are a source of new opportunities and ideas.

- **The Outer Circle (The Energy Guardians):** This circle is not for people, but for boundaries. It defines what and who you need to protect yourself from. List the types of interactions, environments, or relationships you consciously limit your exposure to.

  o   e.g., Negativity, gossip, unsupportive family members, time-wasting activities.

C. Action: Community Investment Plan

A community requires investment.

- **To Strengthen My Inner Circle:** I will_____
  (e.g., Schedule a regular check-in, express my gratitude for them).

- **To Expand My Affiliate Circle:** I will_____
  (e.g., Attend one new networking event or online community this month).

- **To Fortify My Outer Circle:** I will protect my energy by_____
  (e.g., Limiting time on social media, setting a boundary with a specific person).

SECTION V

Integration -
Living the Doctrine

WORKSHOP 13:
Faith & Inner Strength - Anchoring Your Journey

> **Objective:**
> To define your personal sources of inner strength and faith that will serve as an anchor during inevitable storms and struggles.

A. Reflection: Sources of Strength

1. When you have faced your darkest moments, what has pulled you through? Was it prayer, a memory, a person, a core belief?

_____

_____

_____

_____

2. What do you have unwavering faith in, regardless of evidence? (e.g., Your own resilience, a higher power, the goodness of people, the process of growth).

_____

_____

_____

_____

B. Exercise: The Anchoring Statement

An anchor keeps a ship steady in a storm. Create a personal anchoring statement you can return to when you feel doubt, fear, or the urge to quit. It should be a declaration of your core truth.

- **Formula:** "Even when I cannot see the way, I trust in [Source of Faith] and draw strength from [Source of Inner Strength]."

- **Example:** "Even when I cannot see the way, I trust in God's plan for my life and draw strength from the resilience I have proven I possess."

- **My Anchoring**

  Statement:

  _____

  _____

  _____

  _____

C. Action: The Daily Practice

Inner strength is a muscle. Identify one small, daily practice that reinforces your anchor. This could be:

- **Morning Affirmation:** Reciting your Anchoring Statement.

- **Gratitude Journaling:** Writing down three things you're thankful for.

- **Mindful Meditation:** 5 minutes of quiet focus on your breath.

- **Consumption of Wisdom:** Reading a text that aligns with your faith.

- **My chosen practice is:** _____

  _____

  _____

  _____

WORKSHOP 14:
Winning in Relationships

— Objective: —

To apply the "Wired to Win" doctrine to your personal relationships, ensuring they are sources of strength, not sabotage.

A. Reflection: Relationship as a Mirror

1. Which of your current relationships most reflects the person you are becoming? Which one most reflects the person you were?

_____

_____

_____

_____

2. What is one communication pattern you have that you know could be improved?

_____

_____

_____

_____

B. Exercise: The Relationship Balance Sheet

Choose one key relationship (partner, family member, close friend). Assess its health honestly.

- **Assets (What it gives you):** List the positive contributions (e.g., trust, laughter, support, honesty).

  _____

  _____

- **Liabilities (What it costs you):** List the negative drains (e.g., drama, negativity, broken promises, your self-respect).

  _____

  _____

- **Action Plan:** Based on this assessment, what is one specific action you can take to increase the "assets" or decrease the "liabilities"?

  o _Example: To increase assets, I will schedule a weekly date night without phones. To decrease liabilities, I will calmly address a specific broken promise._

  o **My Action Plan:**

  _____

  _____

  _____

C. Action: The "I Feel" Conversation

Using the formula from earlier, have one courageous, honest conversation this week to improve a relationship. "I feel [emotion] when [behavior] happens because [impact]. I would appreciate [request]."

Living Legacy - A Life of Significance

Objective:

To shift the focus from personal success to significance, defining the legacy you will begin building today.

A. Reflection: The Echo of Your Life

1. What is a piece of advice, an act of kindness, or a lesson from someone else that still echoes in your life today?

_____

_____

_____

_____

2. If you were to pass away tomorrow, what is the one-sentence summary people would use about your life? Is that acceptable to you?

_____

_____

_____

_____

B. Exercise: The Legacy Statement

A legacy is not about what you get, but what you give. It's the value you add to the world.

- **Formula:** "My legacy is to use my gift of [Your Core Strength/Talent] to [Your Action of Service] for [The People You Serve]."

- **Example:** "My legacy is to use my gift of storytelling to empower formerly incarcerated individuals for my community."

- **My Legacy Statement:** _____

  _____

  _____

  _____

C. Action: Legacy in Motion

Legacy is built in daily actions. What is one project, habit, or commitment you can start *now* that puts your Legacy Statement into motion? It can be small.

- **Examples:** Mentoring one person, volunteering monthly, creating a resource, starting a blog to share your lessons.

- **My Legacy Action:** _____

_____

_____

_____

_____

_____

CONCLUSION:
Your Wired to Win Life Plan

This is the culmination of your work. This single page is your strategic blueprint. Synthesize everything you've defined in this workbook into this living document. Review it weekly, refine it quarterly, and let it be the compass for your life.

My Wired to Win Life Plan

- **My Vision (The Mountain I'm Climbing):**
  A vivid description of my ideal life and legacy in 5-10 years.

  _____

  _____

  _____

  _____

- **My Personal Constitution (My Compass):**
  My mission statement and core non-negotiable values.

  _____

  _____

  _____

  _____

- **My Anchoring Statement (My Anchor in the Storm):**
  My source of faith and inner strength.

  _____

  _____

  _____

  _____

- **My Victory Goals (The Next Base Camps):**
  My 3-5 primary S.M.A.R.T. goals for the next 12 months.

  1._____

  2. _____

  3. _____

- **My Quarterly Rocks (The Path):**
  The 1-2 key projects for the next 90 days that will lead to my annual goals.

  1._____

  2. _____

- **My Daily Disciplines (The Steps):**
  The 3-5 non-negotiable daily habits that ensure I move forward.

  1._____

  2. _____

  3. _____

- **My Winning Tribe (My Climbing Team):**
  The names of my Inner Circle and my plan for engaging my community.

  _____

  _____

  _____

  _____

- **My Legacy (The Summit Marker):**
  My Legacy Statement and the one action I am taking now.

  _____

  _____

  _____

  _____

This is your doctrine. This is your plan. This is your life. Live it wired to win.

The Journey Is the Destination

You have done the profound work. You have excavated your core identity, forged a vision that pulls you forward, built the disciplines of victory, and equipped yourself with the tools for resilience and leadership. This is not the end of a process, but the beginning of a new way of living.

The principles in this workbook are not a one-time fix; they are a lifelong operating system. The work you've done here has rewired your circuitry, but the power must be continually generated through consistent action. The destination is not a place you arrive at, but a path you walk with intention every single day.

Your Ongoing Victory Protocol:

- **The Daily Alignment:** Each morning, begin with your Daily Declaration. Let your Vision Statement and Personal Constitution be the compass that guides your choices before the world's noise intrudes. Each evening, practice a moment of gratitude for one step taken, no matter how small.

- The Weekly Review: Every Sunday, conduct a brief but honest audit. Ask yourself:

  o **What was my one significant win this week?** (Celebrate it.)
  o **Where did I face a setback, and what did it teach me?** (Reframe it.)
  o **Does my planned activity for the coming week directly align with my core goals?** (Correct the course.)

- **The Quarterly Recalibration:** Every three months, set aside time for a deeper review. Revisit your entire Wired to Win Life Plan. Is your vision still compelling? Are your goals still relevant? Your values will be your anchor, but your strategies must adapt as you grow. This is the sign of a true leader—the ability to lead yourself through changing seasons.

- **The Legacy Check:** Once a year, read the Legacy Letter you wrote to your future self. Are you living in a way that will make that future self proud? This is the ultimate measure of your success.

You did not need to import anything to succeed. You only needed to reconnect with what was already there. This workbook did not give you anything new; it simply helped you remove the corrosion from the winning wiring you were born with.

The final truth is this: **Winning is not a distant summit you finally reach. It is the integrity, courage, and purpose you cultivate with each step of the climb.**

The path is before you. You are equipped. You are prepared. You are, and always have been, wired to win.

Now, go live your proof.